"Identity Crisis" by Ian Macks details the silent inner voice of a black man screaming. Magnifying the "not black enough" trope that's been pervasive in our culture, Ian Macks' poetry reads raw and emotional. Punished and misunderstood, as a black man in America, Ian fires back with poems that are unapologetically black, in words that are meant to be felt not just read. Consumed by colorism projected onto him, Ian Macks spills the tea in this captivating walk through his existence. I encourage you to walk these miles in his shoes. A must-read for anyone who felt alone in a room full of friends.

Kayla Davis

Seeking zero validation, Ian Macks' newest poetry collection "Identity Crisis" is forthright and laid bare. The work sings of his pain and stark realities like cuts made from a razor's edge. Ian upturns the common politesse to find our not-so-hidden assumptions and biases, using his voice to affront the ideologies of our times. "Identity Crisis" resonates with hope and courage, staying defiant through it all—on racism, violence, conformity and hypocrisy from all sides. From a childhood that was spent mostly mute, Ian Macks, now a man, speaks in verses and lines that detonate louder than a bomb.

James Duncan

Speaking candidly about everyday prejudice in his poem "The Generational Cycle", Ian Macks writes "Too bad when you/forget life isn't fair/growing up." These words echo sentiments I found within Ralph Ellison's "On Being the Target of Discrimination", where Ellison states "...Another lesson in the sudden ways good times could be turned bad when white people looked at your color instead of you." Although we live in times of great progress, it's telling to hear similar consensus in Ellison's and Macks' point of view, despite the obvious gaps in history. Throughout "Identity Crisis", Ian Macks boldly tells us how it is, speaking his truth resulting in a memorable poetry collection indeed.

Stephen Furlong

Identity Crisis

ALSO BY IAN MACKS

A Loss and Gain of Comfort

IDENTITY CRISIS

POEMS

BY

IAN MACKS

recto y verso
EDITIONS

PREFACE

This collection of poetry is the truest statement of my identity of twenty-seven years on this earth. This is a salvo for the black child that was non-verbal until five years old, diagnosed with PDD-NOS on the Autistic Spectrum, and written off entirely at ever having the possibility of a functional life. A concerted reply to those who viewed me as an "oreo", "white", "awkward", "cringe", and "fake" once they truly saw me for who I am, not on their assumptions based on appearance and demographics. A contrite rebuttal to everyone complicit in letting me be the fool for their ideals and benefits.

For anyone that's felt these feelings through their life, I hope "Identity Crisis" can relate to you and help give faith that these hardships can also prompt true self-actualization. In our society, suicide among young black males remains a hidden stigma, so much so that law enforcement uses these statistics to their advantage in covering up present day lynchings. We are not allowed to express emotion without also triggering anxiety, defensiveness, and threats. We are told to be patient and vilified when we have the last word, even if it's relevant, truthful, and long overdue.

This oppression of my voice by former acquaintances, colleagues, and partners left me near a state of borderline schizophrenia.

I felt paranoid beyond words, like everyone was out to get me, only to eventually see it was all in my head. Mostly generated ideologies and assumptions from the outside. Being in a state of desperation, feeling a void of acceptance and romantic love ended up leaving me colder, losing a sense of mindset, of who I was and what my life had become. Seeing myself at my worst, taking that step back helped me see how foolish I had been to people around me and my family. Our guilt lays deeply hidden, in either past trauma, drugs and alcohol, romantic love, etc. However this guilt stems from insecurities and a silent fear, to finally feel the weight of time, life, and self-worth.

Therefore, "Identity Crisis" is not directed at anyone specifically, but rather the state of our current times and how it affected my life in the past two years. I never felt like a real adult, in terms of my actions, because they were not yet grounded. This bewildering sentiment has mostly been the folly of my generation; Millennials and Generation Z'ers. We blindly give our faith away to technology, politics, and beliefs but if you're not ready for a reckoning, you'll end up even worse off than before. It's time to rebuild our shattered existence, without sacrificial martyrs, through examining our deeper truth. No matter who you are, I hope you take away something good from this project, in hopes of bettering your life. Temet Nosce.

Iam Maoks

Our Dreams are Kerosene

Witnessing two
racist incidents
on back to back days
in Albany and Troy
respectively could
leave the coldest
human burning alive

The first antagonist
who said:
"Of course you'd
tell me to fuck off."
and the second
who backtracked:
"Not you, them!"

Underlined the harsh reality
that although I'm not a
"Fucking Nigger"
I'm still a nigger
and I need to keep that
in my conscience

Forget that and
I'll end up getting
dehumanized
at the local dive bar

Unless the snow bunnies
bail me out and fetishize
through white lines
in bathroom stalls
Caucasian acquaintances
equals Get Out of Jail
as the monopoly increases
in wages and risk

Can't start the car
cause I rear-ended it
in hot pursuit
of this shit

Yeah, I'm thankful
life hasn't fucked
me up enough
that I can still write

But we all start
forgetting what dreams
are when the alcohol
starts talking
and the weed
puts the world
on mute

Being a good person is
great and all,
but it doesn't erase
the fact

there will
always be
someone
and
something

cherishing the day
you fuck up
or stop fucking
with their existence...

Nevermind, forget it...

I thought about getting
a small coffee
from 'bucks
until I saw my only ex
from high school
and walked away
before she could
recognize me

Initially, it just felt like
I didn't want her to
ask my name
and have a conversation
I'm not in the mood for
Soon, I realized that
it was that I still
couldn't tell her
I wasn't really into her
in the first place

I just dated her
in 10th grade
so my pops
would stop
calling me gay
for never having a
girlfriend

Now she's popping
bagged sammies
and ringing in Ventis
like I was

We didn't need
Emma Willard
or La Salle
to end up
disaffected once
we graduated
past being
together because
our friends were

Conversations with
myself are already
a fucking adventure

I don't miss you,
but I miss feeling
the blank canvas of
youth

When shit I thought was
a chore
was actually
anything but

Rather, a reflection
of ourselves as individuals,
and how we handle
responsibilities

Shake for a bit, then fade
into the background
while it swirls around you
This is the new
Black History

Never realizing who
we are
because we've been
molded to
survive against those
who hold the power of
our chances

Our light is just
a means to an end

I remember how
delusional
my parents thought
her mom was
for putting an island
in her kitchen
cause she never
passed the bar

Who are they to
judge though?

We had to
make our own
islands...

Theatrics

New Year,
same shit,
transparent façade

Crows peck for
their life
on grass and
in garbage cans
Hoping to profit
on humanity
not being on their shit

They're coming in droves
and leaving with success

It's uncomfortable
being in control
of forgiveness
when people wrong you

You soon become subject
to the microscope
Treading more carefully
each step to feel
'safe'

This trend,
looking for scapegoats
when you fuck up,
can't face it

It's not shocking,
yet I'm still petrified
The most accessible,
same humans,
different employees.

They're just having
an off day in their eyes,
but when I'm viewed
in the same lens,
the perception shifts
towards lazy and high

Is this the year America
lines up the crosshairs,
sets the golf ball
of black anguish
on a tee,
to drive off
of society and
sanity?

We've been distracted
with Call of Duty
when our race
is the favorite Battlefield
for the United States

Sinking in place
whilst acting
irate

Oil Changed

It didn't take long
for the fire
to spread

Fully entrenched
an immature passion
that had started
seeping out into
hot takes

Keeping everything
that I'd been holding back
A smoky incineration
of what used to shine bright

You don't do hugs,
I get too deep too quick,
so can we at least
shut it out for a bit?

Can one truly love
fully open
or just a crack

Yeah, I should
probably ask that

The difference between
possessive bonds
versus proper reciprocity

Pundits for agendas
Writers for war-torn
Romantics
Does this poet
even stand?

Just a pessimistic
who conflates hubris
for confidence

This community
and its youth are
breaking right in
front of me
and I've been crying
what I chose not to
change

Slowly,
socioeconomically,
neglected
They wave hello
for a father figure

The real one sits in jail
for drugs low key
protected and served
by those who
protect and serve

The News they want
you to hear
are the apartments,
not the 85% of households
that are single parents

Should've been grateful
that mine tried to make it
work for the betterment of me
but all I could feel was sorry
about old fears and insecurities
A narcissistic evangelist,
the devil has made up
for lost ground

Autonomy Search Party

The search for autonomy
in life can be
polarizing

So many investors
want me to sell
whilst I'm still trying
to gain back
principal control,
broke beyond what's
in my wallet

I could've been anything
but this,
and maybe I could've been
the proper only child
transcending the ego

Money matters more in
United States of Affairs
It took them to a
different social class
I just remind them of
what they left

Not being an affluent
shell of a human
has allowed me
to see everyone
and everything raw

Just put some fucking
respect on this name
and invest in the soul
rather than the sum
or else I'll solve
the equation myself

The Generational Cycle

Consistently judged
and racially profiled,
this perspective has
been suffocating
my whole soul
and I just keep
coughing up bitter

A legacy built
on the foundation of
coping mechanisms:
Class,
Hedonism,
Graduate School,
Food

Feeling bad for my
aunts and uncles
who lost it in
the working class
while my parents
coast in Suburus

Too bad when you
forget life isn't fair
growing up

Hard to be a leader
when nothing is ever
good enough
reigns supreme
in the psyche
Diluting the meaning of
retirement and
a semi-suburban home

Tossed myself out the car,
made a home in the trenches
with an ear to the concrete
and a pen in my hand
and to my name

on the same level
as my aunts and uncles
being ripped for just being
themselves
while Mom and Dad
are starting to actually
go to church
because it's all too
real for them now

They never thought
I'd be with them,
but did they ever
know me?

How could I
define this static?

Now they're
searching for meaning
how everyone else
does it but me

Putting in that work
will be the only
acceptable apology

Independence

Stability

The Ringing in My Ears

When will the
bell stop
taking its toll?

Not even angry
to be honest,
I never really was
Just disheartened
and concerned
that feeling anything
is a privilege I won't have

To do and go through this
just to be reciprocated
in the opposite sense
Manifesting destiny is
difficult
if you're dark

The more I've sold my soul,
the further I've been
stomped down in this life
Living through all this
is the weirdest fuck you
I could give
this city of ugly

They wouldn't wish
a life like mine
on their worst enemy
because we're black
and too smart
for my own good
That's why they rely
upon us to imprison
ourselves

Ghosts of Gentrification

"Keep Grinding."

Thanks, but no thanks

I'd say it's more like
keep rolling,
just like the homeless dude
wheeling across the street
from these downtown churches
abandoned or repurposed

Something flipped inside me
like a derelict property,
refurbished and sold
at a higher price
Is that what we are now?
Selling ourselves
just to be sold in the end
It's scary under bright lights
That's why it's kept in the dark

Not ready to tear apart
Just ready to move
forward,
elsewhere
Internally,
tired of each breath
feeling like meh

Do I have to fight
just to exist again?

But keep the faith,
keep the faith
Follow God like Ye
Just to nail your soul
to the cross…

Ruin the Whistleblower

Get what you can
then get out
It's crazy up here,
you can't get comfortable
I'm not trying to see straight,
just trying to see clear

Light is scarce in stray lights
Attempting to cope with
different demons
Coming up short in
different facets
The pain is immaculate

Whistleblower of
systematic racism
Now I'm holding the ball
in a game of
Kill the Carrier

The start of the
weird season
Where everything feels
harder to do,
but more meaningful
to keep

Not making much,
but making it through
each day

I'll take that for now
and build into the great
that's been
unconsciously paid
through regretful ways

Orbit

Polarized transmissions
from Mars
are what my words
now amount to
"I'm fine, thank you."
as the waitress
pours me coffee anyway

The search to be anything
worth remembering
an isolation
full of life

My support system is
already wondering
if I'll ever be
the same again...

Alienated mindset,
alienated friends

I thought space would
shield me from the world
Instead, it has taken me

A ghost living,
breathing,
haunting loved
ones into prayer

Faith is seldom
and subjective
Pupils dilated,

this has consumed me
What can I even be?

A distress call
fallen on deaf ears

Assessed on the basis
of the system
rather than who I am

Can't even trust
in definitions

Light years deceased
while time still ticks
in seconds

A martyr for the
empathetic human
condition

Weighted Blanket

"Evil."

Having that
stated that about
my psyche
towards her gender
It's jarring

But I couldn't refute it

The verbal weaponry
I utilized when mistreated
by another was hypocritical
at best

A genuinely good soul
that just needed
to believe in
themselves

This misconception,
a cock block
to my father's
personal pursuits

We both share the trait
of fucking up good things
and learning from it eventually,
but he overcame the oppression
while I let it define me

He survived the
projects,
survived the army

It's human nature
to want to
will shit to live,
even when the time
has been up for a while

I've come to grips
with the damages
of being the
vicarious vessel
for this "ideal"
It wasn't because
I fucked his life up

But because
the only way
he could feel
alright is if I could
live a stable life

They tried to lynch him
on Halloween
ESF Ranger School
Class of 1976
tells me I'm attending ESF
when I'm graduating
High School
Class of 2011

Pursued women
who don't
want anything
to do with him
I follow the same tune
Mom shakes her head:
"What's left to you?"

I slowly turn into
Mr. Desperation
Beg and plead to
have a chance
just to rip you to shreds
when you properly
do the math

We just couldn't stop
Now the date is April 2017
and I live on the streets

But the separation had to happen

Being away from
that atmosphere
showed me how fucked
these traits were

How I used the people
I assaulted with words
The same words
that had given me empathy
as a poet

I was truly a pariah
and a living fraud
2011-2020
Practically the entire decade
with nicotine, weed,
and alcohol becoming my IV
I deserve to be single
and completely understand
the skepticism
I encountered when
we were dating

"I love my family,
but they won't understand."
"I love my girlfriend,
but I just wanna fuck her."
These are quotes that
I've heard inside and out
one, two, many times

Now the answer is required
as to if I love myself

There are still concerns
that my career instability
has made their parenting invalid
But I know it's the opposite
Because at least I'm not airing out
my family, friends, and lovers
for pity and acceptance

I'm deconstructing this weight
that has kept me awake
for years

Over the Top, Behind the Back

I used to get called
Nigger and Oreo
from 8th through 12th grade

An old friend would
get in trouble
for sticking up
in my defense

He punched one kid
in the temple
and pushed the other
into a glass chest

He kept this from me so long
An unsaid that spanned a decade
We'd seen each other fall and rise
to numerous occasions
Thought I could trust him
for god knows how long
until we both lost touch
with reality

Barely surviving the
the grey area

Karma is as strange
as brutal honesty

They smile and
make conversation
when I bump into them
but I know they remember
and it still exists within

Operating on these set terms,
cognizant of surroundings,
capturing everything
from those I'm forced
to be around

Reading and sensing
idiosyncrasies
that help them live
without losing it

Their problems
pale in comparison

A pedestal set
on a cracked foundation,
but objectivity and
compassion
are scarce when
you're there

The only
abundant resource
is the ability
to use two faces

Ignore
the privilege
to weigh down
those who are
less fortunate

Return to (soul)

I'm coming back to you

The happy soul
with the opportunity to live
who didn't wake up and say
"What's gonna fuck with
my life today?"
A purpose is forgotten,
or more honestly stated,
felt undeserved

The leaves have fallen
The streets,
they're sopping wet
with tears
My gloves are
beaten to shit,
still picking them up
Sobriety,
a mind that isn't high
It's hitting
all at once
Life

A hernia
without health insurance
A wrist begging to be cut
lacking the blade
A stool without a noose

A broken human
still trying to live
Piece by piece
The search for peace
never ends...

The Mission

I've been tasked with
the toughest mission
of my family tree
The proper handling
of emotions and trauma
before it becomes
a self-fulfilling prophecy

The success rate is pretty low
especially among men

I thought my
three maternal cousins
had it down until:
my favorite one went AWOL
another lost
his throat to a wire cutter
and the last one
took a gunshot wound
on the corner

It's crazy cause the first one
scares me the most

Passing the wounds along,
they've accumulated
on both sides,
and the slit lines
my sternum
with poetic symmetry

A message to
my alma mater's
psych center
and PTSD meditation

I'm in the fetal on the floor
This wasn't a scene from
Leave it to Beaver
where Father and Son
are in perfect harmony

Mom used to tell me
how bad he wanted that
and to tell you the truth
so did I...

A parallel divide
I'm here on the hardwood
whilst he's rocking
on the couch

At least we're both crying
while trying
not to let anyone see

Veins Popping//Inconvenience

Everybody wants to talk about
how Ahmaud Arbery
was shot for a lynching,
but two years prior
He was harassed
by a cop for his
"Veins Popping"

White people always
look for a reason
whether they know Joe
or are
feeling the Bern...

I'm glad that I realized
this scene of assumed stereotypes
didn't want me or my writing
around in the first place
We're just an inconvenience
The unsafe in their safe spaces
The indelible truth of their
cliche niche

They say it's a fine line and
they're sorry when checked,
but knowing the truth
makes them lose their breath
So, for those watching,
praying for me
to become the token
of their cash out dreams

Too bad it's not true
I see your bias for what it is
Have fun in your
upstate utopia,
here's your tolerable "Fuck you."

Homecoming

Becoming reacquainted
with my father's old workplace
Where he held in the anger
that his white coworkers brought
Just to take it out at home
Play a show for the fans
while unconsciously becoming
a caricature

I was headed
in the same direction
Being made an example
in that fashion's worse than
falling on deaf ears

Dealing with selective
listeners still struggling to
define their privilege
or more plainly what
that even fucking means...

So I walk and observe

Wondering how
Mayor Sheehan endorsed
Mayor Bloomberg
Can't wait till I'm
stopped-and-frisked
for walking on Lark Street

The artist who assimilates
will eventually lose their color
Becoming a malleable canvas
to eventually be exploited
and taken advantage of
in silence

Milk

My bones
they can't stop
shaking

"I can't breathe."
The sequel
Central Park Karen
"He's an
African American..."
Yet both shared
a common trait

Race was
all
that
mattered

Black minds
left scattered
Another hashtag,
another protest
We want to give
you
hell

The reply is simple:
"Here's some milk."

Whether it is
a glass
or
a gallon
The tear gas
can't compare
to the tears shed

I shudder at
the thought of
leaving my apartment
while others walk
telling you off
for having to wear
a mask

If only they doubled
as a muzzle

Then they'd feel
how I did when I
was non-verbal

Talk about
slapping a label
to someone's face

Ghosts among me

Inspired
by the front porch
where I grew up

Attempt to sit still,
rocking
back and forth
on the back porch

The birds
chirp symphonies
I attempt to utilize
this sound
to ward off
intrusive thoughts

A familiar cardinal
stares back at me
before flying off
once again...

I'm starting
to understand
what the definition
of guilt and shame
truly mean

If I saw
some of those
faces
ever again,
I'd rip them
a new asshole
and scream a hole
through the ceiling

I wonder if I let my
enemies
get too close

Adages
turn into
omens

These situations foretold
"I needed to listen"
Feeling and seeing this
in heart and mind
burning me alive

I cannot rest
when I can be
laid to rest
with just one
human interaction

White Noise (Renovated)

Beating a dead horse
like Saratoga

If I wear
a dark hoodie,
will I be accosted
and have my life
ended?

Attempts to
quell these fears
have become
the habitual

A crossfaded fog,
pricy exchanges,
fleeting feelings

Any semblance
of controlled volume
surpasses decibels

Welcome to the
Every Day Earthquake

The Richter scale goes
Skittles and Iced Tea
followed by
selling loosies
to forged checks
and autism

Slipping through
the cracks in
increasing magnitude

The Fools

Othello
meets
Romeo and
Juliet

Brought this
on ourselves,
so it's time to
digress

Our brains insane,
so much recovery
on the way

Who won?
No one,
because we
didn't listen;
never listened

This silence,
I'm never
forgetting it
or how this all
broke down

Surrounded by fools
while being one
to shield insecurities
so arrogantly

Protecting doubts
and becoming less
real

Assumptions turn
into division

Say Hello to the Feds

I'm just giving
everything
to moving on
from this prison in
my head
with welded bars
an honest mistake

Crying on social media
who can be trusted
after trusting this,
a hope that led me
to hell on earth

Managed to get a ride
to a fresh start
new and improved
with motives beyond
ego-driven statements
on cracked ideals

Here come the Feds
Blacked out Suburban
Two-faced gatekeepers
Questioning my life
patting me down

The gaslighters
would be so proud,
donning masks of ignorance,
question me as the passenger,
equalling the statements
when this was all over

This messenger
has infiltrated the
bulletproof vest

"My only problem
with you is you're
a Mets fan."

A display
of hypocrisy
on I-90

Two Blind Mice
but I'm seeing
clearer than ever
We were a meme
A bumper sticker
marking our privilege

A reckoning I now
have to live with

Shelter has a
whole new
meaning
Bend, but
never shatter

I'll weld together
my soul to show
you all what
love
means
Those knees
deserve a truth
worth bleeding
for

True liberation
at the expense
of overdue karma

Lost in the Forest

Hidden pockets
of a stable environment
are always cherished
in urban terrain

Beyond offering
a calm escape
They show that
meaning and progress
can coexist anywhere,
in any atmosphere

It feels as if
we're all lost
in a personal forest
stuck in our way

We see glimpses
of clear paths
switching in and out
through covers
of canopy,
broken branches,
fallen trees

Continuing to build
self-worth
whilst family, friends
and creditors
begin to breathe
down your neck

Stretch you out
tied to a board
No flotation
or separation

Week by week,
to be left weak

False strength
isn't a fair replacement
for true weakness

The heart
on this sleeve
is no longer
out entirely

The demons still breathe
once in a while,
lowering the oxygen
through Hennessey
that burns warmth
into these cold veins

I want to make
so many things
better again,
revise all the wrongs,
but I can't feel
like I used to

It hurts
to keep driving
the same point
into the ground
I've replaced this
apathy
with a genuine embrace,
an understanding
this place has
shortcomings
like anywhere else

You can still
find the beauty
in the beat
of a pulse

Even one that's
contained within
the gates of
socio-economic
fragility

An existence that's
rich in color
and wealthy in peace

Fair Trade

Life
is a drug
in its own
right

You can't
ween
off this shit
Lethal emotions
Hypodermic faces
What's the detox?

Distract and disappear

These dark rooms
are still powered
by the outside light
because heartbreak
is more organic
than anyone realizes

Witnessing friendships
decay like compost

Those that swore
they meant the most
dumping you in the
trash and off
like a ghost,
leaving you clung
to the past like velcro

Let go?
Oh no...

A trade
of positive
energy and intent
for the return
of honesty and reality

This pessimist
needs to eat crow

A native son
who can finally
return to the
roots of their
actual home

Believe in
their worth
to transcend
the norm

If you feel that way...

Here are some lines
I've heard for some time
about how
White People
about my life

"If you feel that way."
We'll just keep
watching
while you do
the hard work
of healing

I'm done
concealing
this disappointment
has left me
reeling and
we can't fall for
the trap

Attacking leads
to incarceration

So instead,
Friendships are
incinerated

Don't get too
full of it,
we haven't
made shit
because the
little we do
make is
quickly erased

This list
of ex-acquaintances
comes close to the
length
as black lives
lost

So feel free
to keep looking
for answers
because between
you and me

Every human
finds a way
to feel this way

Open Season

Mental weapons
are far worse
than real ones

They've put
me and others
in positions that
make us the target

When you don't
ask for trouble,
there won't be any

No wonder I
feel attacked on
all sides

If the thoughts
in my mind we're
broadcasted, would
a shrink be flown in
to give me the meds
and be "normal"?

Can't pick the right
battles for shit
A wounded veteran
from the war of mental
health

It's exhausting
to perseverate
over these answers

They love what
makes us this way,
but hate what that
brings along with
it

Used to unpack
the baggage with
my mouth expecting
others to claim it

It's insufferable
to just lay in bed
waiting to disappear
because you're scared
of the outside

Setting myself up
to be the next name
of a protest due to
being mentally gone

Put the hood over my
head and pin me down
to the pillow

Already living
with neurological
bullets in the brain

Two Cents Donation

Let's back
our brothers and sisters
with the blue
that started
it all

Material possessions
attempting to cover
the emotional void
A black hole
lacking empathy
showing no remorse

I don't need
any payment
to be a dominant
switch on their
self-centered
endeavors

They forgot
they were
guests

False voice
sings
too loud

Get Out
before this
weary sob
becomes
a battle cry

Exhausted from
victimizing myself
through fears and lies

Receipts Galore

So many
little instances
peeks between
blinds

Safety in question,
if only I was
not...this

I could
take the heat
without fearing
death

So many
fucking times,
they stare
alienate
and objectify

I remember it
all
Trading brushes
for Dixon
Ticonderogas

Plain and Safe

That's all
that rolls
around here
Gobble it up
without warning
to regurgitate
their true feelings

As the House Show
rages through the night
a neighborhood over
gets locked up,
thrown around,
stomped down
for even less

It's not that hard,
stop standing
indifferently,
please

We have
the receipts
and demand
a return or
exchange

Policy aside,
We will ride
until the end
for a fair
life

The Nightmare of Complacency

The recurring dreams
of what this all meant
will be one of those
battles we have
no choice but to pick

Searching for mirrors
rather than looking
into our own

Don't say what
needs to be said?
Live life dead
"Fought until the end"
we sure did

Life isn't fair and
the double standards
are always there

Forgiveness
is a blessing
in these times
we're living in

Relearn to live again

The mind is a
terrible prison
when the tale
can never be
told
Trying to be
anyone's anything
with a target
on the soul

The Turn

Oh dear,
I was afraid
of this all along

They made the
protest about
their voice,
decentralizing
the vital ones

Now we're rushing
"Back to Normal"
and it's killing us
in more ways that
can ever be explained

Didn't wanna rush,
but real niggas
clapped back,
burst the bubble
Now we see,
this just screamed
trouble

No longer
3/5ths of me,
so let's keep it
one hundred

What happens
when one manifests
without knowledge
of spirit?

Anxiety becomes
reality
Can't shed
the negatives
that can never
be changed

"What was that?"
"Where are you
going?!"

This goes beyond
spiritual bypassing
and realigning chakras

Stats don't lie
and they're all
over the place

Disheveled in
so many ways

Now all I'll hear
is: "You need therapy
and meds."

All those years
of mom working
at a mental hospital
only for her only
child to willingly
lose their head

All I can do now
is prevent her from
visiting me there

Ausente

The distance
is felt
so differently
now

Logistics
paled
in comparison
to emotional
well-being
due to
unpacked trauma

We can't sleep
while we
rest restless

It's how
being awake
has been
this whole time

We thought
not having plans
would make
this unbreakable

Yet we're breaking
before our very eyes

We can't rush
loving and knowing
ourselves first

Yet we'd rather
burn the memory
than face this

Realization

A self-fulfilling
prophecy becomes
a chilling reality

Here comes the
chorus that can
no longer be put
on mute

A possession
driven off of
subjective methods

Appeasement as
crutches for limp
smiles

A trap house
for hearts where
hitting licks involve
Passive-Aggressive shots

All normative claims,
no objectivity,
generalize success

Dirty looks on
The phone and in
person

Trading places from
being a passenger
shotgun to boarding
the Bus

A gallon of Chocolate
Milk, Grapes, and an
8th of Whiskey
boards on the first
stop across the Hudson

Even though it's
"West Troy",
'vliet shares
their priorities

The cul-de-sac
could never
understand

You can't paint
a picture from
distant demands
that you've never
consistently observed

Don't tell me
what I say
and see

That's not love

That's throwing
life away

Farewell, via Lancaster

We knew this
got too big,
couldn't settle
playing house

When we
felt this
our souls
were so
empty

Life has shown
me the reality
but I can't see
your light anymore

The ideal
of being in an
interracial
relationship
is easier than
living it

We need to
let this title go

We're tainting
everything we've
changed properly
just to not
feel secure alone

Why assume
an oppressed identity
just to run
from checking
our own privilege?

Why are we
running from
ourselves
when they told
us so many times
before?

It's starting
to turn
into a
piss take

Our self-worth
is more than
a swipe right
and two weeks
of fuckery

We need to
start drawing
lines for ourselves,
shit's bleeding
out insanity

I'm not a monster

I'm just sick
of never feeling
complete
with you
We need to
complete ourselves
for ourselves

All of this shit
you and your friends
feel at twenty-two
is just a moment
suspended in the
framework of time

Scream it out to you
that I'm turning
twenty-seven and
see all my mistakes,
yet you tell me I'm
distant and threw this
away

Cut open through
Ad Hominems

We can't
run from
life anymore

Keep letting the
pride
have all of us
and it'll end up
being all we
ever have

We should be
living for more,
I don't care if
I have to force
the hand

The separation
for the proper
reunion is long
overdue

Treading

This conscience
breaks the surface
and I realized
in seeing
the privilege
we neglected
I remembered
mine

My family
were exhausted
of how I wanted
to mask this by
bleeding out
for public acceptance

Vibes are irrelevant
when the enabling
still exists

I don't know me
You don't know you
So know this

This is about
the validity
of human life
and the opportunity
of success

Are we alive
to learn and grow
or complain and
moan?

Seeing the
dreamworlds
this society
is giving into

When the trip
ceases in
Midsommar
and she's turning
the Bae Queen

But I've burned
too much
to put on
that bear suit like
Christian
and stitch my
lips shut

This world
is everything
we don't
want to feel,
yet to abuse
empathy for
the game is
crying shame

I'm off
to bring
the sound
for the souls
to lay their
weapons down
and listen

Not for self
but the lost
and forgiven

Seeing the
uncertain shake
with loaded guns
as this life
drifts into
a new unknown

Clinging onto
regret

Faking a smile
to hide
disappointment

The Black Clark Gable

It took a while to
process emotions
with logical thought

Pay attention
to the fine print
before it's all gone

The little things:
A cop enticing
me to jaywalk
on State Street

I show restraint,
he drives away
yelling in his
cruiser

There are a fair share
of hearts that feel
like that frustrated
officer, but I sure as
hell don't give a damn
after putting my own
there

I can love myself
without the whispers
of subjective validation
to twist me

Keep saying:
"I don't understand."

Everything's heightened
right now and
I have to give a damn

Kinfolk

My friends could've
said: "Fuck off,
we told you so."
but they decided
to forgive

They brought me
back,
saved me from
becoming
Tom DuBois,
boondocking
me into
a wake-up call

Never make the
mistake of thinking
this soul will never
listen to their community
that's pushing them
to be better

It brought me back
to the black tree,
where I actually
reside

I'm anxious now
to be welcomed home
with open arms
when I'd been so afraid
of my mind and soul

Cultural Appropriation
goes beyond dreadlocks
and Trauma Porn
no longer gets me off

Cradle Part Two

I'm back
with the
inanimate
objects
that brought
comfort
in lieu
of love

Cooking alone,
making my own
dishes here and
there

It's not perfect,
but at this juncture,
who cares?

It still shakes
me that I was so
internally immobile,
bleeding fuel through
misogynistic pride

Fetishized being the
outcast and believed
the judgments, lost
an identity to the
outside

Why even
twerk it for
me at this
point...

Keep lying
and eating
Takis Fuego?

Rather replace
the spicy gossip
with successful goals

An action
unconsciously
advised against
my knowledge
from false
ideals

Scrolling away
at an opportunity
to know what
it means to
feel

Temptation Island

Back on the
scene again,
dropped the
leash with
a better
read on
relationships

Temptation Island

That's the nickname
which told me how
I'm a tall, dark
handsome red flag

Reality-TV
in real-time,
but I know
it pales in
comparison
to the bigger
picture

Resist
and take
it
slow

It'll be
everything
life could
dream
up

Red Eye

"I've heard stories
like yours before…"

There's this trend
of assumptions here
between white
women and
black men

The latter are
fragile until
they can't be,
then the former
lets us know
how they felt
all along

Exceptions exist,
but they are rare
as shit because
it's either:
"You didn't make
this work."
or
"Suck my dick,
ur dead annoying."

Men like me
are only in charge
when women like
them are sucking
ours

I'd rather be dubbed
honestly than be part
of an interracial fantasy
to get back at bigoted
friends and family

Stigmas baby, Stigmas

13-year-old aspie
shot by police in
Utah
That's Jazz
White on White Crime
but he had autism,
they can't pull a
Warren G and
regulate

His mom cries on the news
So much for a Crisis
Intervention
"Men should be able to
show emotions."

But when they do,
god forbid

Fighting to the end
wasn't a testament
when diagnoses were
double standard

Now we consume
ourselves in movements
that run just the same

Organize and Divide

Can't want Justice for
(Insert Victim Here)
when we're cold too
The ignorant
and illiterate,
signs and all

Seven Shots

Can't even fathom
seven shots of hard
liquor after seeing
them in a black man's
back

The details of these
incidents, specifically
the ones with autism
involved makes
how someone like me
is perceived as a
monolithic problem

A handsome smile
and fresh haircut is
the lowkey armor
we have to keep up

My life can only matter
if I make it such despite
these difficult circumstances
where health and safety are
always on the line

These past seven years,
I took them for granted
and became the living
dead for a while

A second chance
not many get,
usually, it's a
wheelchair
or coffin

My protest ain't
marching alongside
them detached,
saw through that
after a couple of times

It's not fucking
with people that think
they know how I should
be and let the
art speak the mind

Because I don't really
have the sufficient
funds to sue the police
if something happens
to me

Barely hear anyone
say her name these
days...

It's a crying shame,
and this cathartic
expression exploited
in response has never
been a game

How can we expect
them to feel what's
real if they've never
had to fathom the pain

The Life of Humble Pie

This relationship
with myself,
art, self, being
away from the
world that
stripped this life
bare

Polarizing to
the core
of everything
I've been
afraid of:
unconditionally
loving
myself

I understand
this heart now,
avoided the
mental
aneurysm,
drips down the
brain stem

Play the game,
but play for
keeps

Being a bitch
drinking out of
cups
what?
damn...
I was a
narcissistic fuck

Never really there
because the actual
intentions weren't
laid bare

Hello again,
mirror mirror
on the wall

I'm staring this time
even if it leaves
me blind

Never be the same
fool twice

Rebuild from
within
and truly
get this right

Not for me,
but the
greater good
of humankind

For those who
invested in me
while I wasted
my time

Live in Reality

"So now I know
the real from the
fake."

If so, why say it
because that's how
it's drawn in

The feeling is mutual,
and that's not a lie, so
here's the truth

The one where
the "sweetest" black boy
can get nipped and killed
in a Drive-By on
Old 6th Avenue

This is added
to the cuts in his
school district
while the resources
are across the red line

Bleeding colors doesn't
feel so foreign on this
side of the river

Being alive
is more important
than being right
all the time
I need to ensure that
my legacy is more
then a hard worker
and misunderstood mind

Shootouts at Foot Locker

Capitalism in
an insecure world

As if
selling clothes
socially distant
with masks
wasn't fucked enough

The capital city
and the collar city
have taken their feud
to the mall in the 'burbs

Security and Cops
search for who's stealing
when they forgot weapons,
now sneakerheads dodge
bullets for fresh kicks

This pandemic
still has yet to grasp
the reasoning of the
clout reachers,
fake preachers,
and people pleasers

A sense of self-worth
misguided

You need money and
standards for some things,
but at the expense of your
life and soul first?

No wonder we're getting
shelled out for pettiness

A Mother's Love

A portfolio full of
confidential documents

From no words
to too many,
how could I forget
I was never "normal"
to begin with

They only want
Autism to speak
when its a non-profit
that doesn't due the
mental struggle justice

My mom always
offers a way for me
to get medication
besides marijuana

All I can see is how
pills caused friends
and lovers to lose
themselves

Recovery is tough
when you've been
living in a fast car

Beaten across the board
for straying off the
unbeaten path
Forgive me for the
disappointments
I belong thanks to
your unconditional love

Playoffs in August

Aiming higher
in the sky
for a better life,
leaving everything
on the line to define
this mind that's
uncomfortable most
of the time

The same souls
complaining when
you're alive can't
shake the sadness
when you're gone

Responsible decisions
carrying shock value
because suffocating
safety from fear is
the norm

Abusing the misery,
beating that bitch up
until she presses charges
on your mental state

Lawyer up through morals,
discipline, and self-love

Who are they to define
when you've had the
dictionary from the start?
Fill the void internally,
become the champion
of manifesting our dreams,
carrying that trophy eternally

The Power of Responsibility

The capability
to understand the
skills to possess
that give proper
energy

Take that shit
seriously

Errant fun in
shady spaces
doesn't hit the
way it used to

So I stay out of
the fire, observe
from the hill
to avoid another
self-inflicted burn

The fear of missing
out can't equate
to the purpose of
being

Don't pay it
any mind
and be in a
better place
after some time

Cleaning up circles
rounding out squares
Hate it or love it,
still need to care

Quarantined

Talk Therapy:
take three

There's no one
to blame on
quarantine

Looking
in the mirror
less than through
an app or screen

Tried to find
ways to cope
with scary things

Solitude and
the reality it
brings

Singing a tune
no one should sing

Everyone's survived
so many things

How it's processed
is the difference;
soothes or stings

"Stand back and
stand by!"
Are you positive,
my guy?

We took this
country for granted,
just like our lives

IDENTITY CRISIS

POEMS

BY

IAN MACKS

INDEX OF TITLES & FIRST LINES

SPECIAL THANKS

Thank you for reading this story of an identity in crisis, I realize it's a challenge seeing through my eyes, but I hope "Identity Crisis" clarifies how I chose to process my environment and my own existence.

To my best friends, thank you for holding me accountable and showing me how to treat myself better. You are all part of what led me to this point, good or bad, and you helped keep me alive when I really didn't want to be here anymore.

To my former partners, thank you for loving me when it was impossible for me to love myself. You are more to me than words could say, we are the poem I am most proud of regardless of the final outcome.

And to my parents, thank you for your eternal patience through this difficult journey. I couldn't be more proud to be your son. I will never forget the sacrifices made for me to talk, write, and lead a "normal" life. Because of you, I clearly see where I am and what I can become.

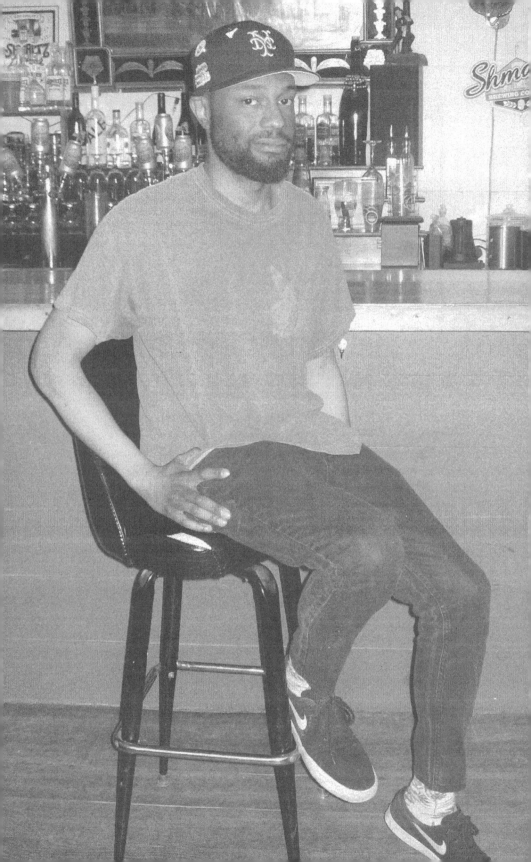

ABOUT THE AUTHOR

Currently based in New York's Capitol Region, poet Ian Macks originally hails from The Bronx, NY. As a youth, Ian was mostly non-verbal during his first decade on planet Earth. These early childhood experiences shaped Ian's emotional sensitivities and point of view on love, loss, racism, and hardship. Ian Macks' distinct poetic voice and literary light shines bright within the poems of his long-awaited sophomore effort "Identity Crisis". Previous work includes Ian's chapbook "A Loss and Gain of Comfort", released in 2014 to much acclaim. Ian Macks performs his poetry at various NY poetry venues such as WAMC's The Linda, Caffe Lena, Brass Tacks, Poetic Vibe, Hudson Valley Writers Guild, Rough Draft Bar and Books, 518 Craft and many more.

This book & other
great work
available
at

recto y verso
EDITIONS

www.rectoyverso.com